14 Sacred Sc...

Low Voice

Edited by Richard Walters

Singers on CD No.1:
*Kathleen Sonnentag, mezzo-soprano; **Kurt Ollmann, baritone

Pianist on the CDs:
Richard Walters

ISBN 978-0-634-08138-5

HAL•LEONARD® CORPORATION
7777 W. BLUEMOUND RD. P.O. BOX 13819 MILWAUKEE, WI 53213

In Australia Contact:

Hal Leonard Australia Pty. Ltd.
22 Taunton Drive P.O. Box 5130
Cheltenham East, 3192 Victoria, Australia
Email: ausadmin@halleonard.com

Visit Hal Leonard Online at
www.halleonard.com

for Sharon

Ah, Holy Jesus

Johann Heermann, 1630
translated by Robert S. Bridges, 1899

"Herzliebster Jesu"
Johann Crüger, 1640
arranged by Richard Walters

Steady, expressive

Ah, ho-ly Je-sus, how hast thou of-fend-ed,

That man to judge thee hath in hate pre-tend-ed? By foes de-rid-ed,

by thine own re-ject-ed, O most af-flict-ed! Who was the

Thy death of an - guish and thy bit - ter pas - sion, For my sal - va - tion.

dolce, rit.

rit.

espressivo

Slower

There - fore, kind Je - sus, Since I can - not pay Thee,

mf warmly

I do a - dore Thee, and will ev - er pray thee, Think on thy pit - y

cresc.

f

mf

and thy love un - swerv - ing, Not my de - serv - ing. ____

rit.

mp

p colla voce

espressivo

8va

Brother James' Air

Based on Psalm 23

James L. Bain
(1840-1925)
arranged by Brian Dean

lead - eth me, the qui - et wa - ters by. _____
bless - ed - ness E'en for His own name's

2. My sake. _____

Yea, tho I walk through

shad - owed vale, yet will I fear no ill, For Thou art with me

and Thy rod And staff me com-fort still; Thy rod and staff me

com-fort still, me com - fort still. _____

My ta - ble Thou hast fur-nish-ed in

pres-ence of my foes. My head with oil Thou dost an-noint, And

Amazing Grace

John Newton (1725-1807)

Early American Folk Melody
arranged by Richard Walters

fear, And grace my __ fears re - lieved; _____ How prec - ious __

cresc.

mf

did that grace _____ ap - pear The __ hour I _____ first be - lieved. _____

decresc.   *mp*   *decresc.*   *p*

3. The Lord has __ prom - ised good to

mp

me His word my __ hope se - cures; He will _____ my __

poco. cresc.   *mf*

*The singer is encouraged to embellish the melody; small notes are stylistic suggestions.

shield and por - tion — be as — long as — life en -

decresc.

dures. _____ 4. Through

mp

p

pp

mp

man - y — dan - gers toils and snares I have al -

read - y come; _____ 'Tis grace _____ hath — brought me

8va---------- 8va ---

safe ____ thus ____ far, And grace will _ lead me home. _____

5. Yea, when this ___

cresc.   *mf*

flesh and heart shall fail, And mor - tal ___ life shall

cease, _____ I shall ___ po - sess with - in _____ the ___

Than ___ when ___ we first be

gun. ___

Was blind ___ but now I see. ___

* A third vocal line option:

Than ___ when ___ we first be - gun. ___

Ave Maria

Franz Schubert

A -   ve Ma - ri -   -
A -   ve Ma - ri -   -

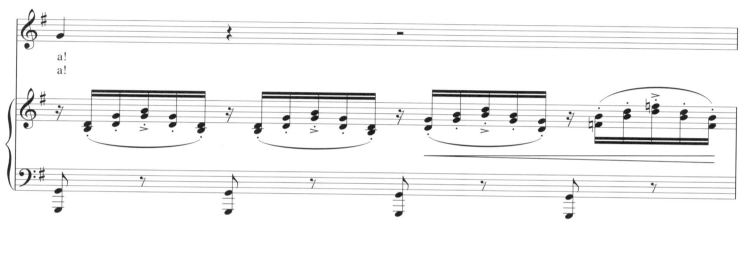

a!
a!

sim.

dim.

Balm in Gilead

Jeremiah 8 : 22

African-American Spiritual
arranged by Harry T. Burleigh

The Call

George Herbert

Ralph Vaughan Williams

Deep River

African-American Spiritual
arranged by Harry T. Burleigh

camp - ground. Deep _____ riv - er, my home is o - ver Jor - dan _____ Deep _____ riv - er, Lord, I want to cross o - ver in - to camp - ground. Oh, don't you want ___ to go _____ to that

gos - pel _____ feast, _____ That prom - is'd land _____ where all _____ is peace? Oh deep _____ riv - er, Lord, I want to cross o - ver in - to camp - ground. _____

How Can I Keep from Singing

American Folksong
Arranged by Richard Walters

Allegretto; steady

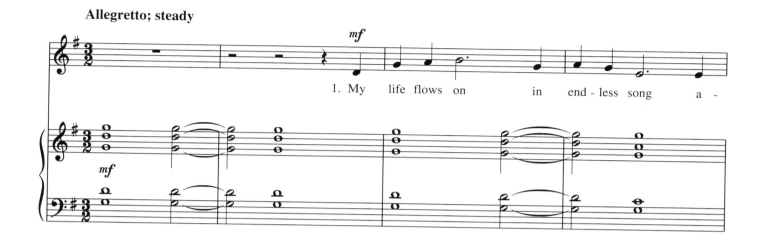

1. My life flows on in end-less song a-

bove earth's lam - en - ta - tion. __ I hear the real, though far off hymn that

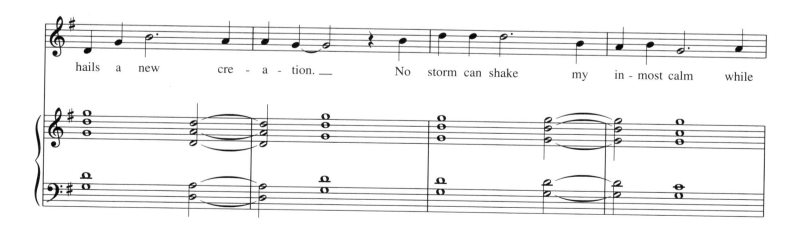

hails a new cre - a - tion. __ No storm can shake my in - most calm while

to that rock I'm cling-ing. __ Since love is lord of __ Heav'n and earth How

can I keep from sing-ing? __

mf warmly

When ty-rants trem - ble, sick with fear And hear their death knells

like a sturdy hymn

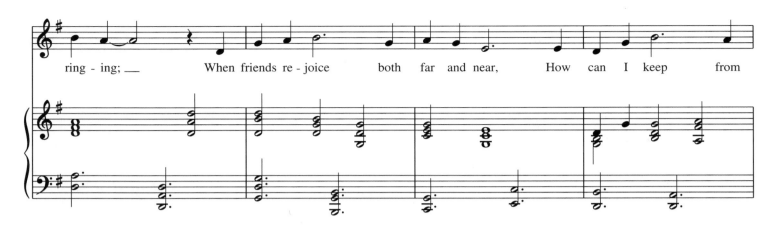

ring - ing; __ When friends re - joice both far and near, How can I keep from

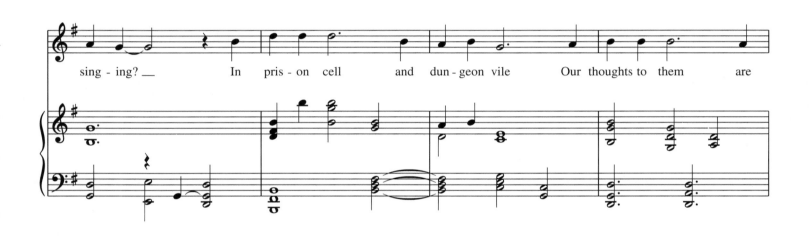

sing - ing? __ In pris - on cell and dun - geon vile Our thoughts to them are

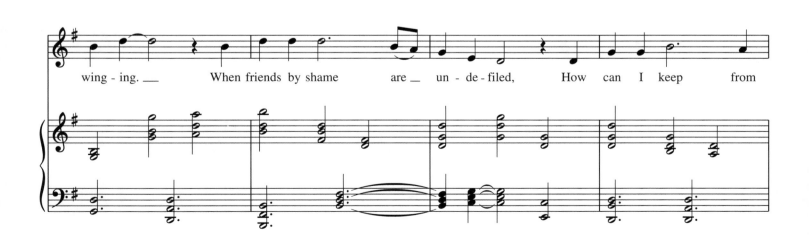

wing - ing. __ When friends by shame are __ un - de - filed, How can I keep from

sing - ing? __ No storm can shake my in - most calm while to that rock I'm

Slower to the end

cling - ing. __ It sounds an ech - o __ in my soul. How can I keep from

sing - ing? ___ How can I keep from sing - ing? ___ How

can I keep from sing - ing? ___

Jesu, Joy of Man's Desiring

Johann Sebastian Bach
Arranged by John Reed

Lyrics:
Je- su, joy of man's de- sir- ing,
Ho- ly wis- dom,
Through the way where hope is guid- ing,
Hark, what peace- ful

Because of length, a singer may choose to perform just verse one. This has been the case on the companion CD.

Love ___ most ___ bright,
mu - sic ___ rings!

Drawn by Thee, our souls as - pir - ing
Where the flock, our in Thee con - fid - ing,

Soar to un - cre - a - ted ___
Drink of joy from death - less ___

light.
springs.

Word of God, our flesh _____ that fash - ion'd
Theirs is beau - ty's fair - est plea - sure,

mf

With the fire of
Theirs is wis - dom's

p

cresc.

throne.
known.

Sheep May Safely Graze

from Cantata No. 208

Johann Sebastian Bach
adapted by Christopher Ruck

If the piece feels too long for your church service purpose, two options may be employed:
end at the "Fine" before proceeding to the "B" section; or rather than "D.S. al Fine" at the end of "B,"
repeat back just to the last four bars before "Fine". The recording repeats back to the 𝄋.

Last time

Fine

p

f

p

1st time

(*tr*)

He who rules with vi - sion guid - ing ____

Brings us ____ rest and peace a - bid - ing, ____

pp

p

Saves our souls from __ end - less __ night.

He who __

rules with vi - sion __ guid - ing, __ Brings us __

rest and peace a - bid - ing, Rest

and peace, Rest

and peace a - bid - ing,

D.S. al Fine

Saves our souls from end - less night.

Just a Closer Walk with Thee

Traditional American Song
arranged by Richard Walters

We Are Climbing Jacob's Ladder

African-American Spiritual
arranged by Richard Walters

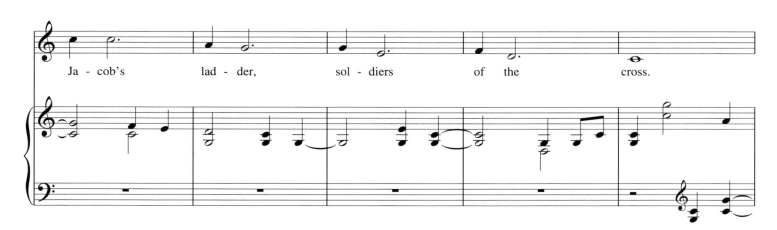

Espressivo, rubato

3. Do you think I'll make a good sol-dier? Do you think I'll make a good sol-dier? _____ Do you _____ think I'll _____ make a Chris-tian sol-dier _____ sol-dier _____ of the cross?

Poco piú mosso

We are climb - ing Ja - cob's lad - der, we are climb - ing Ja - cob's lad - der, we are climb - ing Ja - cob's lad - der, sol - diers of the cross.

sub. *p*

(*p*)

8va

Wondrous Love

American Folk Hymn
arranged by Richard Walters

When I was sink-ing down, O my soul, O my soul, When

I was sink-ing down, O my soul, When I was sink-ing down He

lay a-side His crown, He lay a-side His crown for my soul, for my

soul, He lay a-side His crown for my soul.

p

legato

mp   *mp*

soul, What won - drous love is this that _____ (opt.)

caused the Lord _ of bliss to bear the dread - ful

curse for my soul, for my soul, to

bear the dread - ful curse for my soul, _____

Wayfaring Stranger

Southern American Folksong
arranged by Richard Walters

This song seems like a spiritual, and it may well be one, but those origins have been unconfirmed.

3. I'll soon be free from ev-ry tri-al, my bod-y

sleep in the church-yard. I'll drop the cross of self de-

ni-al and en-ter on my great re-ward.

I'm go-in' there to see my Sa-vior, to sing his